This Journal Belongs To A Millionaire Name

_____

Date:

I am confident in my ability to make tough business decisions.

I am attracting loyal and repeat customers who are advocates for my business.

I am worthy of success and prosperity as a small business owner.

I am resilient, overcoming challenges with grace.

I am making a positive impact with my small business.

I am worthy of financial abundance and prosperity through my business.

I am building a scalable and sustainable business model.

My small business is contributing positively to my community.

Date:

I am a visionary leader, guiding my business to success.

Date:

I am capable of adapting to changing market trends and consumer needs.

I am nurturing a strong and loyal customer base for my business.

I am resourceful, finding creative solutions to problems.

I attract loyal and satisfied customers.

I am confident in my ability to innovate and stay ahead in the market.

I am confident in my products/services and their value.

Date:

I am confident in my marketing efforts and promoting my business with pride.

I am building a reputable brand and reputation for my small business.

I am setting clear and achievable business goals and working towards them.

I am attracting the right partnerships and collaborations for my business.

I'M A
Resilient
BUSINESS
OWNER

I am providing value and excellence in everything my business offers.

My business is an asset that brings me financial abundance.

I am a capable and successful small business owner.

I make wise decisions that benefit my business.

Date:

I am effectively managing my business finances and investments.

Date:

I am constantly seeking opportunities for growth and expansion in my business.

My business is thriving and growing every day.

Date:

I am confident in my ability to market and promote my business effectively.

I am creating meaningful and lasting relationships with my customers.

My business is thriving and growing.

I am a successful small business owner.

Date:

I am taking care of my physical and mental well-being to excel in my business.

I am committed to providing exceptional customer service in my business.

I am worthy of receiving support and assistance in growing my business.

I am constantly improving my products/services to meet customer needs.

I am confidently promoting my business and its unique value proposition.

I am constantly learning and improving as a business owner.

I am creating a positive and inclusive work environment for my team.

I make
WISE
Business
DECISIONS →

I am taking consistent action towards achieving my business goals.

Date:

I am grateful for the opportunity to create a positive impact in the world.

I am a confident and effective leader for my team.

I am a skilled marketer, promoting my business effectively.

I am open to learning from failures and using them as stepping stones to success.

I am celebrating every small milestone and success in my business.

I am continuously learning and improving as a small business owner.

I am effectively utilizing my resources and maximizing my business potential.

I am capable of overcoming any challenges in my business.

I am focused and disciplined in managing my business operations.

I am confident in my ability to overcome obstacles and achieve my business vision.

I am confident in my unique business offerings.

Date:

I am continuously expanding my customer base.

I am attracting positive reviews and testimonials for my business.

I am creating a positive and supportive work culture for my team.

I am attracting abundant opportunities for my small business.

I am organized and efficient in managing my business.

I am attracting loyal customers who value my products/services.

I RECEIVE OPPORTUNITIES FOR Growth

Date:

I am attracting and retaining top talent in my business.

I am building strong partnerships and collaborations to drive business growth.

I am worthy of financial success and abundance.

I am surrounded by a supportive community that uplifts my business.

I am deserving of recognition and praise for my hard work.

I am a risk-taker, willing to step out of my comfort zone for my business.

I am a visionary, creating a clear path for my business's future.

I am committed to providing exceptional customer service.

I am a problem solver, finding solutions to business challenges.

Date:

I am persistent and determined, never giving up on my business goals.

I am a strategic planner, setting achievable objectives for my business.

I am skilled in managing my finances and making sound financial decisions.

I am building a reputable brand that resonates with my target audience.

I am confident in my unique value proposition that sets my business apart.

I am a relationship builder, fostering meaningful connections with my customers.

I am a continuous learner, staying updated with industry trends and best practices.

I am grateful for the opportunity to pursue my passion through my small business.

I am a positive influencer, inspiring my team and customers with my mindset.

I am resilient in the face of setbacks, bouncing back stronger.

Date:

I am a leader who leads by example, setting high standards for my business.

Date:

_____

_____

_____

_____

_____

_____

_____

_____

_____

_____

_____

_____

_____

_____

_____

_____

_____

_____

_____

_____

_____

_____

I am effective in managing my time and prioritizing tasks for my business.

I am worthy of success and prosperity in my small business journey.

I am a goal-setter, setting clear and achievable goals for my business.

Date:

I am committed to continuous improvement and innovation in my business.

I am confident in my marketing strategies, attracting and retaining loyal customers.

I am an expert in my industry, providing value through my products/services.

I am a creative problem solver, finding unique solutions to business obstacles.

I take
CALCULATED
RISKS

I am a leader who empowers and motivates my team for success.

I am a strategic thinker, making informed decisions for the growth of my business.

I am confident in my business plan and strategies for long-term success.

I am worthy of financial abundance and prosperity in my small business.

I am a go-getter, taking action to achieve my business goals.

Date:

I am a trusted advisor to my customers, providing valuable solutions.

I am resilient in the face of competition, standing out with my unique offerings.

Date:

I am a networker, building valuable relationships for my business.

I am a problem solver, finding efficient solutions to business challenges.

I'M
BUILDING A
Reputable
BRAND

Date:

I am confident in my abilities and committed to the success of my small business.

My business is growing and thriving.

I am capable of overcoming any challenges that come my way.

I am confident in my business skills and expertise.

I am a resilient and determined entrepreneur.

My hard work and dedication are paying off in the success of my business.

I am worthy of the success and prosperity my business brings.

I am skilled at managing my finances and making wise business decisions.

I am surrounded by a supportive network of mentors and fellow business owners.

I am creating a legacy through my small business.

I am worthy of charging fair prices for my products/services.

I am confident in marketing and promoting my business.

I am capable of adapting to changing market trends and customer needs.

Date:

I am attracting new opportunities and partnerships for my business.

I am persistent and tenacious in pursuing my business goals.

I am grateful for the flexibility and freedom that owning a small business provides.

I am confident in my ability to scale and expand my business.

I am creating a positive work culture within my business.

I am making a difference in my industry with my unique offerings.

I am worthy of success and recognition as a small business owner.

I am focused and disciplined in managing my time and resources.

I am building a loyal customer base that trusts and supports my business.

I am a leader in my field, setting a high standard for excellence.

Date:

I am constantly innovating and improving my products/services.

I am open to learning from failures and using them as opportunities for growth.

I am building meaningful relationships with my customers and stakeholders.

I am taking calculated risks to grow my business and achieve my goals.

I am worthy of taking time off to rest and rejuvenate for the success of my business.

I am constantly seeking feedback and learning from my customers and peers.

I am confident in my unique value proposition and what sets my business apart.

I am creating a positive brand image through consistent branding and messaging.

Date:

I am building a loyal and engaged online community for my business.

I am embracing change and adapting my business strategies accordingly.

I am confident in my ability to make wise investments in my business growth.

I am creating a legacy that will benefit future generations through my business.

I am confident in my ability to balance work and personal life for overall well-being.

I SET CLEAR AND ACHIEVABLE GOALS

I am grateful for the support and encouragement of my customers and community.

I am constantly seeking ways to improve customer satisfaction and loyalty.

I am building a strong and reliable team that shares my vision and values.

I am confident in my ability to lead and inspire my team towards success.

My small business is successful and thriving.

I am a confident and capable small business owner.

I am attracting loyal and satisfied customers.

Date:

I am making a positive impact in my community through my business.

I am a skilled entrepreneur, navigating challenges with resilience.

I manage
FINANCES
EFFECTIVELY

I am continually learning and growing as a business owner.

I am a strategic planner, setting clear goals and achieving them.

I am creative and innovative, finding new ways to grow my business.

Date:

I am a decisive decision-maker, making wise choices for my business.

I am building a strong and reputable brand for my business.

I am effectively managing my time and resources for optimal productivity.

I am confident in my products/services and their value to my customers.

I am adaptable and flexible, adjusting to market changes and trends.

I am setting realistic expectations and surpassing them in my business.

I'm worthy OF FINANCIAL ABUNDANCE

I am building a loyal and committed team to support my business.

I am overcoming challenges and obstacles with resilience and determination.

Date:

I am celebrating my achievements and milestones as a small business owner.

I am confident in my unique strengths and expertise as a business owner.

Date:

I am building a strong online presence for my business.

Date:

I am providing exceptional customer service that sets my business apart.

I am building a diverse and inclusive business that reflects my values.

I am making wise financial decisions to ensure the sustainability of my business.

I am embracing innovation and technology to stay ahead in my industry.

I'M RICH
Powerful,
AND
INFLUENTIAL

I am staying focused and disciplined in achieving my business goals.

I am building strategic partnerships to expand my business opportunities.

I am attracting and retaining top talent to support my business growth.

I am managing my business with integrity and ethical practices.

Date:

I am constantly seeking feedback and insights to improve my business.

I am effectively managing my business finances and resources.

I am building a positive reputation and brand image for my business.

Date:

I am seizing opportunities and taking bold actions to grow my business.

I am grateful for the support and patronage of my customers and clients.

MONEY
FLOWS
FREELY
Towards
ME

Date:

I am staying true to my business values and mission.

I am attracting abundance and prosperity to my small business.

I am a forward thinker, anticipating and preparing for future business trends.

I am building a strong and loyal customer base for my business.

I am resilient and persistent, never giving up on my business dreams.

I am staying focused on my unique value proposition in the market.

I am building a supportive network of fellow entrepreneurs and business owners.

I am a positive influencer, spreading optimism and motivation to everyone around me.

I am building strong partnerships and collaborations to drive innovation and creativity in my business.

I'M NOT LIMITED BY THE OPINIONS of others

I am a beacon of positivity, spreading joy and happiness through my business.

I am a risk-taker, embracing challenges and turning them into opportunities.

I am a role model, showing others what is possible through hard work, determination, and passion.

I am a mentor and guide, helping my team members grow and succeed.

I am a firm believer in my own potential, knowing that I can achieve greatness in my business.

Date:

I am a steward of my business, nurturing it with care and attention to ensure its success.

Date:

I am a customer-centric business owner, always putting my customers first.

Date:

I am a lifelong learner, constantly seeking knowledge and improvement for my business.

I am a builder of relationships, nurturing meaningful connections with customers.

I FORGE MY OWN path to SUCCESS

I am a leader who leads by example, inspiring my team to be their best selves.

Date:

I am inspiring and uplifting those around me with my entrepreneurial spirit.

I am a goal achiever, setting and reaching ambitious targets for my business.

I am a motivator, encouraging and empowering my team to reach new heights of success.

I am a magnet for opportunities, attracting abundance and prosperity into my small business.

Date:

I am a trailblazer, blazing a path of success for others to follow in the world of small business.

I am a visionary thinker, always looking ahead and planning for the future of my business.

I am a learner for life, constantly upgrading my skills and knowledge to stay ahead in the market.

I am a go-getter, taking action every day to achieve my business goals.

Date:

I am a role model, inspiring others with my success as a small business owner.

Date:

I am a magnet for success, attracting abundance and prosperity into my business.

I am a go-to expert in my field, trusted and respected for my knowledge and expertise.

Date:

I am a dream chaser, never giving up on my vision for my business.

Date:

I am a solution-oriented business owner, finding creative ways to overcome challenges.

I am a strategic thinker, making informed decisions to drive the growth of my business.

I am a great communicator, effectively conveying the value of my products/services.

Date:

I am a trailblazer, paving the way for other small business owners to follow.

I am an expert, sought after for my knowledge and expertise in my field.

Date:

I am a game changer, disrupting the status quo and creating new possibilities in my industry.

I AM A Creative FORCE

www.ingramcontent.com/pod-product-compliance
Lightning Source LLC
Chambersburg PA
CBHW082145120626
46553CB00010B/2769